THE NATURE LIBRARY

WILD ANIMALS

DAVID ALDERTON

CRESCENT BOOKS

NEW YORK

This 1991 edition published by Crescent Books,
distributed by Outlet Book Company, Inc.,
a Random House Company, 225 Park Avenue South,
New York, New York 10003.

Printed and bound in Hong Kong

ISBN 0-517-05156-7

8 7 6 5 4 3 2 1

Library of Congress Cataloging-in-Publication Data
Wild animals
    p. cm – (Nature Library)
  Includes index.
  Summary: Examines the day-to-day life of a wide variety of wild
mammals.
   ISBN 0-517-05156-7 : $6.99
  1. Mammals – Juvenile literature.   (1. Mammals.)   I. Series.
QL706.2.W55 1991   90-41151
599 – dc20   CIP
                                          AC

Credits
Edited and designed: Ideas into Print, Geoff Rogers and Stuart Watkinson
Layouts: Stonecastle Graphics Ltd.
Picture Editors: Annette Lerner, John Kaprielian
Photographs: Photo Researchers Inc., New York
Commissioning Editor: Andrew Preston
Production: Ruth Arthur, Sally Connolly, David Proffit, Andrew Whitelaw
Director of Production: Gerald Hughes
Director of Publishing: David Gibbon
Typesetting: SX Composing Ltd.
Color separations: Scantrans Pte. Ltd., Singapore

The Author
David Alderton has had a life-long interest in wildlife. Since graduating
from Cambridge University, his work as a specialist writer on animals has
enabled him to travel far afield, observing many creatures in their natural
habitats. David also attends various international meetings where
conservation matters are discussed, and he is acutely aware of the
difficulties faced by many species today in their constant battle for survival.

CONTENTS

Above: Vicunas grazing on the High Andes in Peru. These elegant creatures, related to the domesticated llama, have long been valued for their fine wool, particularly by the Incas. Today, they are protected and their numbers are increasing again after a dramatic fall during the 1960s.

Left: The curious pygmy hippopotamus, found in the forests and swamps of West Africa. This species reaches about half the length and a tenth of the weight of the larger one. Note the sticky secretions from the skin glands.

LIONS – THE KING OF BEASTS

One of the best known members of the cat family, the lion is now confined to parts of Africa and a tiny area of India, although they used to occur right across Africa and southern Europe into Asia. The last European lions were killed in about 100 A.D., and since then, the range of the 'king of beasts' has contracted even further in Africa itself.

Lions live in groups called 'prides', made up of one or more males – recognizable by the longer mane of hair around their necks – and perhaps 20 lionesses and young cubs. Hunting is a cooperative venture, with the male generally preferring to feed off the lionesses' kills, and so reserving his energies to drive off potential rivals. Lions take a variety of prey, preferring larger animals such as zebras, although when food is short, they will catch hares, birds and even small rodents. Lions have also been known to eat fruit.

Lions make formidable predators, especially in a group. Approaching from different angles, they can sprint at speeds of 58kph(36mph) over short distances,

moving as close to their target as possible before revealing their presence. Regular kills are essential to the well-being of the pride, with lionesses each requiring 5kg(11lb) of food every day, while lions need 7kg(15.4lb).

People are most likely to be killed when the lions are hungry. Having acquired a taste for human flesh, however, lions will then carry out further attacks. A particularly bad situation of this type arose during the construction of the Uganda railway in 1898, when lions persisted in attacking workers in the vicinity of Tsavo.

Below: Two lion cubs playing together, all part of their natural development. Their mother teaches them the necessary hunting skills for their survival.

Left: Asiatic lions have declined to the point of extinction. This lioness is one of a group bred in captivity. Lions used to range as far north as the UK.

Left: A pair of lions drink at a water hole in Kenya. They are far more gregarious by nature than other large cats. While some prides establish territories, others follow herds of game.

Right: A mother with her young cub. Weaning takes place when cubs are about six months old. As many as half the youngsters born will have died by two years old, frequently from starvation.

Above: Lionesses are usually responsible for hunting. They will prey on virtually any creature, but wildebeest are most often taken. Generally speaking, the lionesses avoid the largest animals, such as rhinoceroses and elephants, but giraffes do fall victim to lions.

Lion
Panthera leo

Distribution: Across most of Africa south of the Sahara, apart from areas of rainforest. Also, a tiny population still survives in the Gir Forest Sanctuary in northwestern India.
Size: Males average 1.2m(4ft) at the shoulder; females are smaller, at 1.1m(3ft 7in).
Pregnancy: Up to 17 weeks.
Lifespan: About 15 years in the wild, but can be over 20 years in captivity.
Conservation status: Almost extinct in Asia, but remains relatively numerous in Africa.
Danger element: May attack on occasions, and this behaviour can become habitual, making such lions very dangerous.

Left: A male lion pursues a lioness as a prelude to mating. There is a strong hierarchy in a pride, and dominant males are constantly under threat from the challenge of younger individuals. Males are mature by two years, but may not start breeding until they are five years old. Young males first join up in groups and then take over a pride. Individual males may then remain dominant for up to three years.

Right: A splendid male lion, sporting its characteristic mane of hair. This first becomes evident in male cubs at one year old, starting to grow on the sides of the neck. An interesting behavioural difference between lions and lionesses is that only the females generally climb trees. This may be a reflection of their smaller size, although males will climb a tree fork to steal a leopard's kill.

TIGERS – SOLITARY KILLERS

Tigers are the largest members of the cat family and are found in parts of Asia, where they live in areas of open forest. Unlike lions, they do not live in groups, but have a solitary life style. They establish their territories by various means, not unlike those used by domestic cats. For example, they will scent mark various locations with urine and scratch prominent trees to establish their domain. A male will detect when a female nearby is in breeding condition, and only then is she encouraged to enter his territory. They may stay together for less than two weeks.

Tigers prey on relatively large animals, such as wild deer, although they will also take smaller creatures, even locusts if there is a swarm in the vicinity. Tigers hunt mainly at night, to lessen the likelihood of detection, and may travel considerable distances to achieve a kill. They may be successful in only about one in twenty attempts, and do not eat every day. Studies suggest that, on average, a tiger on its own will make up to 50 kills a year, enabling it to feed about once every eight days. The tiger will drag dead prey off and conceal it in the undergrowth, and return to feed on it over a period of several days until the carcass has been stripped of meat.

The black striped markings of the tiger help to conceal it in undergrowth, by breaking up its body outline. Black tigers have been recorded, while the paler coat of the Siberian tiger ensures that it remains well concealed in the open, often snowy landscape.

Unlike many cats, tigers prove good swimmers, and are not reluctant to enter water. But they are not often seen in trees, and avoid climbing whenever possible. Their hearing is particularly sensitive, helping them to locate potential prey in the dark.

Above: A tiger stands over its kill. These cats hunt alone, largely under cover of darkness, and prefer larger prey such as buffalo. They can consume up to 30kg(66lb) of meat at once.

Below: A white tiger in India. Tigers of this colour are well known in Rewa State, where the Maharaja began to breed them in 1951. They can now be seen in zoos around the world.

Above: The Siberian race of the tiger may well be found in areas where the temperature falls at night to about -32°C(-25°F). When they lie on the snow they are protected by thick belly fat.

Left: A tigress with her cub. Young tigers are born with stripes, but are paler overall than adults. Their coloration darkens by six months of age, and they will also have ceased suckling by this time. They eat meat at eight weeks.

Tiger
Panthera tigris

Distribution: Parts of India, Indonesia, China, Siberia and Manchuria.
Size: About 91cm(36in) high at the shoulder and a head-body length of 1.4-2.8m(4ft 7in-9ft 2in).
Pregnancy: About 15 weeks.
Lifespan: Around 15 years, often longer in captivity.
Conservation status: Now considered to be endangered.
Danger element: Man-eating tigers are known, but as a rule these large cats are very shy and avoid human contact.

Left: As a rule, tigers avoid people, but man-eaters have proved dangerous animals.

Above: A Siberian tiger cub. The coloration of this race, notably in winter, is quite pale.

CHEETAHS – THE FASTEST ANIMALS ON LAND

The cheetah has an astonishing acceleration that enables it to reach a speed of 87kph(54mph) in just three seconds from a standing start. This is close to its maximum speed of 90kph(56mph), although cheetahs may occasionally even exceed this figure in short bursts. Such speed enables cheetahs to outpace their prey, which is largely made up of small gazelles, hares and birds such as bustards, although they will occasionally resort to larger prey, including ostriches and zebras. Cheetahs are not equipped for sustained running, however, and will give up the chase within a minute if it has not been successful. Even an experienced adult will only make a kill once in every two attempts. To maximize their chances of success, they normally stalk their target, perhaps for several hours, in order to get close enough to launch themselves from a distance of less than 30m(100ft).

Cheetahs live and hunt on their own, although occasionally a pair may be seen seeking prey together. After mating, the cubs are born in long grass or hidden under a bush. Three form the average litter, although as many as eight have been recorded. At this stage, they measure just 30cm(12in) long and weigh up to 300gm(11oz). It will be at least five weeks before the cubs can start to accompany their mother when she goes hunting. They will be able to live on their own from about nine weeks, although many cubs die at an early stage, frequently from starvation.

Although they have been hunted in the past for their skins, cheetahs remain relatively numerous across Africa, especially where their habitat is intact. Elsewhere throughout their range, particularly in Asia and the Middle East, their numbers have fallen to the verge of extinction.

Left: Cheetahs are remarkably streamlined animals, which obviously helps them to run at speed in pursuit of their prey. Cheetahs live alone, with a range that may extend over 102sq. km(39sq. miles).

Cheetah
Acinonyx jubatus

Distribution: Centred on Africa, extending via the Middle East to southern Asia.
Size: Measures up to 2.19m(7ft 4in) in length including the tail, which is up to 84cm(33in) long.
Pregnancy: Lasts 13-14 weeks.
Lifespan: Up to 12 years, generally longer in captivity.
Conservation status: Reasonably secure in Africa, but almost extinct elsewhere.
Danger element: Fast, lithe hunter.

Above: A female and her cub playing. Such games help the cub learn to wrestle prey.

Below: The cheetah in pursuit of prey. It will need rest following this tremendous physical effort.

Bottom: A group of cheetah cubs. Nearly half of all cubs are likely to die before maturity.

Right: The cheetah's keen eyesight enables it to recognize prey at a considerable distance. This gives the cheetah the opportunity to move close to its prey before using its devastating pace to outrun its victim.

Left: Resting on the ground, a cheetah remains alert. Even a minor injury may spell disaster and lead to starvation.

Above: Gazelles are a favoured prey of the cheetah, but these cats also take smaller game, such as ostrich chicks and hares. They may drag prey to the cover of a thorn bush, while they recover from the chase.

PUMAS – AMERICAN 'LIONS'

These powerful cats are capable of leaping a distance of over 6m(20ft) on the ground, and may jump 4.6m(15ft) up into a tree. They also have considerable stamina, travelling distances of up to 80km(50 miles) a day when hunting. Deer form the bulk of the puma's diet, although they also feed on smaller animals, including porcupines. A puma often leaps down onto its unsuspecting prey, dispatching it with a fatal bite to the throat. Then it drags its victim to a more secure place to feed on the carcass. Other animals, such as bears, may be attracted to the scene of a puma's kill, and are sometimes allowed to join in the feast. Pumas may attack and kill farm livestock, and this has led to conflict with man. Dogs are traditionally used to hunt pumas, driving the cat up into a tree where it can be shot. But pumas are not dangerous to people, although their ghostly and alarming screamlike calls will carry a long distance at night.

Pumas normally live solitary lives and come together only briefly for mating, which can occur throughout the year. Up to four cubs are born. They are blind at birth, and differ from adults by having spots on their fur and dark rings around the tail. Although the youngsters will be weaned by the time they are three months old, they may stay with their mother for as long as two years. Their coat changes to that of the adult as they mature, although there is considerable variation in adult fur coloration throughout their wide range. As a result, over 30 different subspecies have been recognized. In some areas, the puma is better known as the cougar or mountain lion.

Above: These normally solitary creatures wander over a large area, rarely staying in one place.

Puma
Felis concolor

Distribution: Extends from Canada south to Patagonia in southern South America.
Size: Up to nearly 2.4m(8ft) long including the tail, which can be 91cm(36in).
Pregnancy: Lasts 13-14 weeks.
Lifespan: Up to 18 years.
Conservation status: Some of the 30 subspecies are seriously endangered through habitat changes and hunting.
Danger element: May injure people (specially rabid animals).

Above: The puma can exist in virtually any type of terrain, provided that some cover is available. It is an opportunistic hunter, taking a range of prey.

Right: Nocturnal by nature, the puma is also one of the most secretive large cats. However, if prey is short, it may be forced to hunt during daylight hours.

Above: Pumas will hunt in water as well as on land. Their prey depends mainly on where they live and on the time of year.

Above: A puma in pursuit of a snowshoe hare. It has a relatively poor sense of smell and hunts mainly by sight, although its hearing is also acute. It may stalk its chosen target, moving as close as possible before launching into a strike, or leaping down onto it.

Above: Breeding can take place at any time of the year. A female remains on heat for about nine days. Her scent will be followed by as many as five males, who pursue her ardently. The young will eat meat from six weeks old.

Right: The puma looks not unlike a large domestic cat. Rumours of escaped pumas in parts of the UK have yet to be confirmed, despite sightings.

LEOPARDS – STEALTHY HUNTERS OF THE NIGHT

The name 'leopard' comes from the old belief that these cats were hybrids, resulting from the cross-breeding of lions (hence 'leo') and 'pards', which was another name for panther. The name 'panther' has been applied to several of the larger wild cats in the past, but is now simply used as an alternative name for the leopard. Part of the confusion arose because certain leopards – especially in the Asiatic part of their range – lack the typical lighter markings, and are predominantly black. For a long time, it was believed that these were a different species, and so they were called 'black panthers'. In fact, a study of their coats shows that the darker spotted patterning is still visible.

Leopards are found over a wider area than any other wild cat, but they are shy by nature and thus rarely seen. These cats live on their own, usually preferring to hunt at night, and resting out of sight in dense undergrowth during the warmest part of the day. Leopards can be encountered in virtually any type of terrain where some cover is available.

They will take a very wide variety of prey, ranging in size from dung beetles to large antelopes. Smaller mammals, such as hares and rodents, are generally favoured by younger leopards and older individuals no longer agile enough to deal with large prey. Leopards are skilled climbers, and frequently pounce on animals such as impala from above, inflicting a mortal blow with their teeth.

Evidence shows that some leopards acquire a preference for certain types of prey. This may range from fish to dogs and even people; once a leopard has become a man-eater, it is potentially a very dangerous animal. Like other spotted cats, leopards have been heavily hunted for their skins but, although they may have declined in some parts of their range, the species is not endangered at present.

Above: Leopards are solitary hunters, taking advantage of tall grass and other cover to conceal their presence before striking. In parts of Africa, their main prey are deer, such as this impala.

Above: A leopard drinks from an African river. It must remain ever alert, because in this situation it is at risk from crocodiles. The leopard may also be taken by tigers, lions and wild dogs.

Left: The distribution of the leopard, like that of other large cats, has declined significantly during recent years. They are highly adaptable by nature, but an accurate assessment of their numbers has always been difficult, because they are so shy and elusive. Interestingly, leopards such as this one in the Masai Mara Game Reserve in Kenya, East Africa have tended to reveal themselves more, as they are protected from hunters.

Left: Young leopards are born in a den, with an average litter consisting of two or three cubs. The female cares for her offspring alone, and weaning takes place at three months old.

Left: A black, or melanistic, form of the leopard. Animals of this colour are far more common in Asia, especially in areas of thick forest, where their coloration helps to conceal them. Black leopards are born alongside normally coloured offspring.

Below: The leopard is a highly agile cat. It will climb trees without difficulty, running back down the trunk like a domestic cat. It can run at speeds of about 60kph(37mph) and also swims well. Leopard calls are rarely heard, except at night; those of males are said to be deeper. Leopards may live close to humans without being detected.

Right: This map shows that the leopard can be found across a wide area of Africa and Asia. It is shy and hunts mainly at night, however, and so is rarely seen during the daylight hours.

Leopard
Panthera pardus

Distribution: Africa, mainly south of the Sahara, and in southern Asia. Also present in parts of North Africa, Arabia and China.
Size: Up to 81cm(32in) at the shoulder; males larger than females.
Pregnancy: Lasts 13-15 weeks.
Lifespan: At least 12 years in the wild, longer in captivity.
Conservation status: Widespread, but considered vulnerable.
Danger element: May attack people, and this can be habitual in some individuals.

WOLVES – WORKING AS A TEAM

The likely ancestor of the domestic dog, grey wolves have a wide area of distribution and once roamed over almost the entire Northern Hemisphere. A combination of hunting and increasing urbanization has virtually eliminated them from western Europe, but they remain fairly common further east in the Soviet Union, as well as in North America.

Because they inhabit such a vast territory, wolves from different areas may differ significantly in coloration, with some being much paler than others. Their size is also variable, with individuals weighing as much as 80kg(177lb) having been shot in Alaska, whereas the small grey steppe wolves from Asia may weigh only 12kg(27lb).

Although they live in packs, wolves generally mate for life, forming a strong pair bond. Pack size is influenced by the area and the prey that the wolves generally take, since large animals like moose are dangerous for just a handful of wolves to attack. In these areas, the average pack is likely to consist of at least 20 individuals, whereas, elsewhere, this figure may fall to six or seven. The pack inevitably selects young, aged or sick prey, since such animals are easier to catch and kill, putting up minimum resistance.

Wolves will cover vast areas in search of food, communicating with each other by howling. They establish territories, which vary in area according to the availability of prey. Incursions into the territory of a neighbouring pack are likely to be greeted with an aggressive response. Young wolves leaving a pack in search of a mate, for example, are particularly vulnerable and may be killed rather than accepted by another group. They keep very much to themselves at this stage, and rarely reveal their presence by howling until they are certain of a favourable reception.

Above: Wolves move through their territory mainly under cover of darkness. The size of the territory depends to a large extent on the availability of prey within the area. In most packs, only the dominant male and female will mate. Breaking away from a pack, a young mature wolf, joined by a mate, may establish a new territory, which gradually increases in size.

Right: Differences in both size and coloration have become apparent between different populations of wolves, as they occur over such a vast area. But in many parts of their former range, wolves have been hunted to extinction. They disappeared from the UK in the seventeenth century, and are very localized elsewhere in western Europe, but more common in Asia.

Left: Howling in the snow, a grey wolf keeps in touch with other members of the pack. The calls of wolves are audible to people over distances of up to 16km (10 miles), each lasting from 3-11 seconds. This behaviour also warns other packs tempted to cross into their neighbour's territory.

Left: A female wolf in China nurses her pups. Births take place in spring, and the young are born blind and deaf. They grow rapidly and leave the den at three weeks old. The female regurgitates meat from her stomach for them.

Left: Deer are a favourite prey of wolves, depending to some extent on the area concerned. By hunting co-operatively, the pack can take much larger prey than would be possible for an individual wolf. Occasionally, they may also scavenge.

Right: This young grey wolf cub, faces an uncertain future. Once weaned, at about six weeks old, cubs start to move around the territory, covering distances of up to 8km(5 miles) at a time. If prey is scarce in the winter, cubs often die from starvation.

Right: It is generally accepted that the grey wolf is the ancestor of all today's breeds of domestic dog. The process of domestication may have started in India or China at least 10,000 years ago, although earlier claims have been made. Although considered to be a danger to man, there are few documented cases of wolves attacking people, but they have been known to prey on farmstock.

Grey wolf
Canis lupus

Distribution: Across most of the Northern Hemisphere, although now largely extinct in western Europe.
Size: About 66-81cm(26-32in) at the shoulder.
Pregnancy: About 9 weeks, with an average litter of seven cubs.
Lifespan: Ten years in the wild, but may be up to 20 years in captivity.
Conservation status: Still quite common, although eliminated from urban areas.
Danger element: May attack people occasionally, and can transmit rabies.

AFRICAN HUNTING DOGS – RELENTLESS IN PURSUIT

African hunting dogs are found across the grasslands and open woodlands of Africa. They live in packs, generally made up of about eight individuals, but groups of 20 have been recorded. Each pack roams over a large territory, perhaps extending over an area of 2,000 sq. km (770 sq. miles), and they can travel up to 50km(31 miles) each day. They hunt during the relative coolness of the early morning or the late afternoon, locating their prey mainly by sight rather than by scent. Once they have spotted their quarry, they chase it over a considerable distance at speed. Hunting dogs have been known to maintain speeds of 50kph(31mph) for distances of 5.6km(3.5 miles), and their stamina enables them to run continuously for up to an hour.

Their prey depends to some extent on the area concerned. Wildebeest and Thomson's gazelles are generally favoured in the Serengeti, although some packs here prefer to hunt zebra. The pack will target young or feeble individuals because these animals are easier to catch, being less likely to have sufficient stamina to outpace the dogs. Having dragged down the prey, the dogs rapidly dispatch it and all members of the pack will have an opportunity to feed.

When food is readily available, mating is likely to occur between the dominant male and female. The pups are subsequently born in a den, venturing above ground for the first time when they are about three weeks old. They are weaned by the time they are two and a half months old, and then fed and protected by the pack members until fully independent, about a year later.

Above: Ever alert, an African hunting dog looks for prey on the Serengeti plain. These dogs rely heavily on their sense of sight and keen hearing to detect quarry, and for communication.

Below: At the scene of a successful kill, the pack congregate around a wildebeest carcass. Hunting dogs single out weak or young animals that are likely to tire rapidly and are therefore easier to catch.

Left: Fighting between pack members is not uncommon, especially at breeding time. Bitches battle each other more ferociously than dogs to establish dominance. Only one female in the pack will mate.

African hunting dog
Lycaon pictus

Distribution: Across most of Africa, to the south of the Sahara.
Size: Up to 75cm(30in) at the shoulder.
Pregnancy: Lasts about 10 weeks.
Lifespan: About 10 years.
Conservation status: Considered to be endangered.
Danger element: Not a threat to people.

Below: The hunting dog is entirely carnivorous and armed with a powerful array of teeth. At a kill, the puppies are allowed to eat first, thus increasing their chances of survival. Most packs need to make at least one kill every day. However, these dogs have themselves been heavily hunted because they pose a threat to domestic livestock, and their total population is believed to have fallen to as few as 10,000 individuals. Increasing urbanization has adversely affected populations in some areas, while the disease distemper has taken a toll.

Below: In a pack of hunting dogs, there are invariably more males than females. This is partly a direct reflection of the birth rate, but the fact that males fight less is another explanation.

It is the bitches that tend to leave the herd on maturity, whereas the dogs stay behind and also help to protect the offspring. This is an unusual strategy in carnivores.

Below: A pack of hunting dogs disturbs a group of giraffes. They are unlikely to tackle an adult giraffe, but may well attack a youngster. When prey is short, they will even resort to catching small rodents.

BROWN BEARS – DECEPTIVE POWER

The brown bear is found in areas of eastern Europe and Asia, as well as in North America, making it the most widely distributed of all bears. The largest individuals are found on Kodiak Island, and nearby Afognak and Shuyak, in the Gulf of Alaska. These giants can measure over 2.4m(8ft) along the back, making them a fearsome sight when they rear up on their hind legs. They may weigh as much as 533kg (1,175lb), but in spite of their bulk, brown bears can sprint for short distances at speeds of 56kph(35mph).

These bears inhabit fairly wild areas, where there are few people. They live on their own, or in small groups, foraging for a variety of foods. As well as hunting mammals such as deer, they will catch fish, wading into rivers to scoop up migrating salmon returning to their spawning grounds. Plants and berries also play a part in a bear's diet, and they even use their powerful claws to scrape honey from the nest of wild bees.

When winter approaches and food becomes scarce, the bears will seek out caves where they can hibernate. Their body fat nourishes them through this period. Here, females give birth to their cubs during the late winter, emerging from the lair with their offspring during the early spring.

Attacks by brown bears on people are not unknown, and since a single blow from one of its paws can kill even a large buffalo (bison), these animals are exceedingly dangerous if cornered. In most cases, however, they will avoid people, but they may be attracted to camp sites and rubbish dumps where they will scavenge for food, and this can cause serious problems.

Left: Mother and cub will stay together for two and even three years. Two mothers with their cubs occasionally join up to form a small group that shares responsibility for the litters.

Above: A female with her cubs. Each one weighs less than 0.45kg(1lb) at birth and there may be up to four offspring, but the average is two. They stay close to their mother, who defends them ferociously. Roaming adult male brown bears attack youngsters and may even kill their mother. Wolves are another danger. The young mature quite rapidly and females may breed for the first time when only four years old. However, it may be four years before they produce a second litter. It can take up to 11 years for some males to reach full size.

Left: Young brown bears frolic in the McNeil River, Alaska. Their sharp teeth, claws are flexible paws are clearly visible here.

Above: Brown bears readily take to water, but must learn how to make a catch. They may take up to a dozen large fish.

Below: A Himalayan brown bear. The actual coloration of the coat can vary from blond to black, within its range.

Above: Brown bears are able to walk for a short distance standing on their hind limbs, but normally move on four legs.

Left: The brown bear is known locally by many different names, including the grizzly bear.

Brown bear
Ursus arctos

Distribution: Parts of Europe, Asia and North America. Used to occur in northwestern Africa, but became extinct there during the 1850s.

Size: Males are generally larger than females, with a head and body length of over 2.4m(8ft).

Pregnancy: Lasts 6-9 months.

Lifespan: Over 25 years in the wild, and can exceed 50 years in captivity.

Conservation status: Declining in many parts of its wide range, especially in parts of Europe such as northern Spain.

Danger element: Regarded as the most dangerous mammal in the United States and elsewhere within its range.

POLAR BEARS – DEADLY HUNTERS OF THE NORTH

Confined to the frozen north, polar bears are quite at home on ice floes and will swim readily in the chilly waters. Polar bears wander widely, covering distances of 20km(43 miles) in a day. They can outpace reindeer on land, bounding over the ice at speeds of 40kph(25mph) for short distances, and are able to leap 3.7m(12ft) across crevices. Their coloration helps them to blend in with their background, enabling them to ambush the seals that form the basis of their diet in this inhospitable environment. They prefer areas where there is open sea, since seals will move back and forth onto the ice. Polar bears may take the seals on the ice or seize them in the water. They use their keen sense of smell to track down likely prey, and several may be drawn to the large carcasses of whales. Generally, however, polar bears live on their own.

Polar bears mate in the spring, with the male locating receptive females by their scent. The pregnant female retires to a den dug in drifting snow at the end of the year, just before the cubs are born. Up to three offspring may form the litter, each newborn cub weighing about 650gm(23oz). By comparison, an adult male polar bear can weigh as much as 650kg(1,437lb). Nourished by their mother's milk, the cubs grow rapidly, and will have grown to about 10kg(22lb) when they first leave the den in March. They stay alongside their mother until they are nearly two and a half years old, and she will not breed again until the third year.

Polar bears are generally accepted as being among the most dangerous mammals, and will readily attack people. In turn, however, excessive hunting has seriously reduced their numbers. An international treaty is now established to ensure the survival of this species, although limited hunting, notably by native people, is still permitted.

Below: In spite of their bulk, polar bears are surprisingly agile. They will dive for food and can also swim well, covering as much as 95km(60miles) without stopping, by paddling with their front paws. Their scientific name means 'sea bear'.

Left: A group of polar bears resting close to the port of Churchill in Manitoba, Canada. This town is located directly on the traditional migratory route of the polar bears. Every autumn, they pass very close to the town of about 800 people. A special warning system has been set up to avoid conflict, as some bears enter the streets. Up to 30 are captured and kept in a special pen until the bay freezes over. They are tranquillized, taken by helicopter to be released at a suitable spot and are then able to set off to hunt for seals.

Above: Although they generally live on their own, polar bears do occasionally come together. Young cubs that have left their mother may remain as a group for a time, before splitting up and going their separate ways.

Right: This map clearly shows the distribution of the aptly named polar bear. It is perfectly at home in these vast ice fields.

Polar bear
Ursus maritimus

Distribution: Throughout polar regions in the Northern Hemisphere.
Size: Males can be 3m(9ft 10in) long, females 2.5m(8ft 2in).
Pregnancy: About 8 months.
Lifespan: Can be up to 25 years.
Conservation status: Has declined because of widespread hunting.
Danger element: The most dangerous of the bears.

Above: This bear, feeding on a young walrus, will probably eat the bulk of the carcass. Polar bears have cavernous stomachs and can consume 70kg (154lb) of food at a time. Seals are a favoured prey, but if the ice thaws, bears hunt on land for reindeer.

Right: Studies have shown that the average polar bear probably tracks over an area of 259,000 sq. km (100,000 sq. miles) during its lifetime. It can run at 40kph (25mph) for short distances, but is more likely to plod along at just 4kph(2.5mph). Its broad feet enable the bear to walk easily through thick snow.

Above: A polar bear with snow in its dense coat. Interestingly, the actual hairs are hollow and trap ultraviolet light from the sun. This passes to the skin, is converted to heat and helps the bear to retain its body heat.

GIANT PANDAS – SYMBOLS OF CONSERVATION

The unmistakable black-and-white giant panda is confined to areas of bamboo forest in the provinces of Kansu, Shensi and Szechwan in southwestern China. The species only became known in Europe during 1869, when it was discovered by the French missionary Père David. Since then, the giant panda has captured public imagination like no other animal and has been adopted as the symbol of the World Wide Fund for Nature (formerly the World Wildlife Fund).

Giant pandas feed mainly on bamboo, and have specially adapted front paws for this purpose. One of their wrist bones is enlarged and acts rather like a thumb, enabling them to guide lengths of bamboo between their paws. On occasions, giant pandas also eat other vegetation, and may sometimes catch insects and rodents.

It is their dependence on bamboo that threatens the survival of the giant pandas, because as part of its growth cycle, the bamboo dies off after flowering. Deprived of their natural food, and with the bamboo forests much reduced in area, giant pandas regularly face starvation, and they can no longer move to new areas of forest. Their current population is thought to be as low as 500 in the wild, but increasing numbers are being bred in zoos, both in China and elsewhere.

Giant pandas live on their own, only coming together during the breeding season in April and May. Males and females find each other by scent, although they also call more extensively at this time. The pair split up immediately after mating. The resulting young pandas are tiny at birth, weighing as little as

Above: The giant panda was first thought to be a bear, but then doubts arose and it was linked with the raccoons. However, recent studies again suggest a closer relationship with bears.

100gm(3oz), and it will be about seven weeks before their eyes are open. Weaning takes place when they are six months old, although they will probably stay with their mother until nearly a year has passed.

Left: Giant pandas depend on bamboo forests for their food and survival. As these areas are cleared, so the pandas face increasing isolation.

Right and far right: A female panda nurses her cub, but this 1978 birth was unusual. It was the first breeding achieved by artificial insemination at Beijing Zoo in China. Now, increasing numbers of pandas are bred in zoos around the world, offering hope for their survival.

Above: Pandas are most likely to be seen either at dawn, or in the early part of the evening.

Below: Although bamboo forms the bulk of the pandas' diet, they also eat bamboo rats.

Below: Pandas are unlikely to breed until at least five years old. Populations increase slowly, even under ideal conditions.

Above: Bamboo, is the only food readily available in the giant panda's range. Its leaves contain about 16 percent protein; the panda may need 38kg (84lb) of bamboo daily.

Giant Panda
Ailuropoda melanoleuca

Distribution: Restricted to bamboo forests in southwestern parts of China.
Size: About 70-81cm(27-32in) at the shoulder, with males being bigger than females.
Pregnancy: Up to 21 weeks.
Lifespan: Known to be 20 years in captivity, but may be shorter in the wild.
Conservation status: Bordering on endangered.
Danger element: In spite of its cuddly image, the giant panda is a close relative of the bears, and can use its sharp teeth and claws to inflict serious injury.

ELEPHANTS – THE LARGEST LAND ANIMALS

Elephants are found in parts of Africa and Asia, with the African elephant being the largest of all living land mammals. The most gigantic individual of this species ever recorded was a bull (male) shot on November 7, 1974 in southern Angola. Standing over 4m(13ft) tall, it weighed an estimated 12.25 tonnes (just over 27,000lb). The average height of the African elephant is about 3.3m(10ft 10in), with the Asian species being smaller, and rarely exceeding 3m(9ft 10in).

In spite of their fearsome size, elephants are herbivores, feeding on plants. They need to consume a vast amount every day, with each individual elephant eating around 150kg(330lb) of food and drinking about 80 litres(140 pints) of water. They feed using the trunk, which is formed by a fusion of the nose and the upper lip. This enables them to pull down branches that otherwise would be out of reach, but is sufficiently sensitive to allow them to pull off individual leaves.

Elephants drink through the trunk, sucking up water and squirting it into the mouth. They also use the trunk as a shower hose. Regular bathing keeps their skin in good condition, and helps them to cool down under the hot rays of the tropical sun.

Elephant families live in herds made up of cows with young calves, headed by an old cow that may be at least 50 years old. Bulls tend to wander on their own, or form loose groups, only joining a herd of cows for periods during the breeding season. Sadly, the numbers of African elephants have fallen dramatically during recent years. Poachers have slaughtered tens of

Above: The unmistakable image of an African bull elephant.

thousands with high-velocity weapons for their ivory. In many areas of Africa, elephants have been wiped out completely, and in spite of protection they face an increasingly uncertain future.

Left: Two young bull elephants spar playfully with each other. When they reach puberty, at about 14 years old, they are driven out of the herd and form loose associations with other young bulls, or live alone.

Right: A herd of African elephants wades across a river. They wander far afield in search of food, guided by the senior mother of the herd, who knows the territory well. She may also be the oldest group member.

Above: The Asian elephant can be identified by its smaller ears and less prominent tusks; tusks are usually absent in cows.

Above: The young elephant uses its mouth to suckle from its mother's two mammary glands, situated behind her front legs.

Above: Unlike the youngsters, adult elephants feed and drink with their trunk. It is also used as an effective shower hose when bathing.

Above: An elephant using its tusks to dig in the ground for essential minerals. These are likely to be in short supply in its regular food.

Left: A group of elephants congregate at an African water hole. Here they bathe to keep their skin in good condition.

African elephant
Loxodonta africana

Asiatic elephant
Elephas maximus

Distribution: Africa and Asia.
Size: The African elephant measures about 3.3m(10ft 10in) and the Asian about 3m(9ft 10in) at the shoulder.
Pregnancy: Lasts 17-25 months (22 months average).
Lifespan: Up to 70 years.
Conservation status: Both have declined in numbers, with the Asian elephant being the more endangered species.
Danger element: Bulls are particularly dangerous during the mating period and cows defend their youngsters fiercely.

RHINOCEROSES – PLANT-EATING BATTLE TANKS

Five species of rhinoceros still survive. In the past, there were others, such as the woolly rhinoceros that lived in Europe until the end of the last Ice Age, some 15,000 years ago. Rhinos are now confined to parts of Africa, where the white and black rhinoceroses live, as well as Asia, home of the other three species. The most widespread of these is the Indian rhinoceros, with the Javan and Sumatran rhinos being restricted to these two islands, off the coast of Southeast Asia.

One of the distinguishing features of all rhinoceroses is the horn, the size and number (one or two) of which varies according to the species. The horns are used to deter predators; a charging rhino is a formidable adversary, especially the white rhino, which is the heaviest at 2,300kg(just over 5,000lb). Sadly, the horns have also proved the major reason for their decline. They are highly valued in the Arab world to make dagger handles, while in the East, powdered rhino horn is prized for its supposed medicinal purposes, and commands a higher price than gold.

In spite of their fierce appearance, all rhinos are herbivores, grazing on grasses, plants, shrubs and, occasionally, fruit. They rarely venture far away from water, where they will regularly wallow, coating their bodies in damp mud. When dried, this helps to keep biting insects and parasites off the skin. Rhinos have very limited eyesight, but a keen sense of smell. They generally live on their own, but sometimes females and young calves are seen together, even after the weaning period has passed.

Left: A charging black rhino is a frightening sight, attaining speeds of 45kph(28mph) over several kilometres. It detects possible danger by its keen sense of smell, and will attack both vehicles and people.

Above: A black rhino with her calf. Mating can occur at any stage during the year and the young calf, weighing about 20kg(44lb) at birth, is suckled for two years. It remains with its mother until it is 3.5 years old.

Right: Red-billed oxpecker birds remove ticks and other parasites from a white rhino and her calf at a water hole.

Left: In spite of their ferocious appearance, all five species of rhinoceros are herbivores. The black rhino shown here is the commoner of the two African species. It is less often seen in groups than the white rhino, but does not appear to be highly territorial by nature.

Right: Hunting the rhinoceros for its horns has brought this magnificent beast to the verge of extinction. Effective protection is difficult and costly.

Right: Asiatic rhinos are in even greater danger of extinction than their African relatives.

Rhinoceroses
Family Rhinocerotidae

Distribution: Scattered through parts of Africa, India and Southeast Asia.
Size: Ranges from about 1.4m(4ft 7in) to 1.9m(6ft 3in) at the shoulder; length up to 4m(13ft).
Pregnancy: From 7 to 16 months, depending on the species.
Lifespan: Up to 40 years.
Conservation status: The Asian species are all endangered, and those found in Africa have declined seriously in numbers during recent years.
Danger element: A charging rhino is a very dangerous animal.

HIPPOPOTAMUSES – AFRICA'S RIVER HORSES

The name hippopotamus means 'river horse', although these large amphibious mammals are more closely related to pigs than horses. Found in the rivers and lakes of Africa, the hippopotamus is forced to spend most of the day immersed in water, because water rapidly evaporates from the surface of its surprisingly thin skin at a much faster rate than in other mammals. It used to be thought that hippos sweated blood because of the red droplets seen on their skin, but this secretion from skin glands is simply a means of protecting the surface from becoming sunburnt; hippos lack proper sweat glands.

In spite of their rather gentle and cumbersome appearance, hippos have a pair of daggerlike canine teeth in their lower jaws, and on occasions, males will battle with each other fiercely for territorial rights. These teeth are up to 50cm(20in) long, and together can weigh 2.1kg(4.6lb). In spite of inflicting horrific injuries in some cases, such encounters rarely prove fatal, and the wounds soon heal uneventfully.

At night, hippos emerge on land to browse on grasses and similar plants, which they crop with their broad mouths. Since each hippopotamus needs an average of 40kg(88lb) of greenstuff a day, destruction of the vegetation in some areas where hippos are numerous can result in soil erosion.

Hippos mate during the dry season, with the youngsters being born following the onset of the rains, which ensures a good supply of vegetation and hence milk flow in the female. Young hippos weigh about 42kg(93lb) at birth, and live on their own with their mothers for the first two weeks of life. The smaller pygmy hippopotamus, encountered in forest areas of West Africa, has a similar lifestyle to its larger relative, although it appears to spend less time in water.

Below: In spite of their rather placid appearance, hippos will sometimes fight viciously. Territorial battles between males can last for up to 90 minutes.

Left: Hippos are quite at home under water, where their sensitive skin is protected from the hot rays of the sun. They can remain totally submerged for up to five minutes, and prefer to come onto land at night.

Hippopotamus
Hippopotamus amphibus

Distribution: Through much of Africa, south of the Sahara in suitable areas of water.
Size: Up to 1.4m(4ft 7in) tall and 3.45m(11ft 4in) long.
Pregnancy: About 34 weeks.
Lifespan: Can be at least 45 years.
Conservation status: Still reasonably common throughout their range.
Danger element: Unpredictable, with sharp teeth.

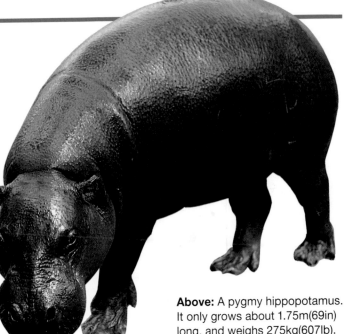

Above: A pygmy hippopotamus. It only grows about 1.75m(69in) long, and weighs 275kg(607lb). Its larger relative can weigh as much as 3,200kg(7,072lb), in the case of the biggest males.

Below: The ferocious canines in the hippo's lower jaw are clearly visible here. These teeth are largest in male hippos, but even females may use them to inflict nasty wounds if they or their calves are threatened.

Above: A mother hippo and her calf. The single youngster is usually born on land, and is able to walk after about five minutes. A young calf sometimes climbs onto its mother's back when she is in the water. This may offer protection against crocodiles.

Below: Mud wallows are often home to hippos. They allow the animals to extend their feeding range, away from larger areas of water. Males often congregate in the smaller wallows. In such localities they are vulnerable to hunters who kill them for meat.

CAMELS – SHIPS OF THE DESERT

The two different species of camel can be distinguished by the number of their humps. The Arabian camel, descended from the dromedary, has a single hump, whereas the Bactrian camel has two. These humps act as fat stores, enabling camels to survive for days without eating. They are also well equipped to survive dehydration, producing a concentrated urine and able to withstand a level of water loss from their bodies that would prove fatal to us. When camels find a water hole, they are able to drink at an amazing rate, consuming as much as 100 litres(27 gallons) in just ten minutes. This is absorbed almost directly into the body. Desert plants help to meet their water requirements when no fresh supply is available.

Camels are kept in a semi-domesticated state throughout much of their range, and have earned the nickname of 'ships of the desert' for their tireless service as carriers of goods and passengers. The Arabian camel is believed to be a domesticated form of the dromedary, which was brought to Arabia and has since colonized this region. Camels are highly adaptable creatures, and the descendants of those taken to Australia during the 1800s to cross this continent's arid interior still thrive there today. Camels are also regarded as bad-tempered animals. They can inflict a very painful bite, and will also spit if annoyed.

Under normal circumstances, a male camel will usually live in the company of several females. Baby camels are born at an advanced stage of development; they are able to walk properly within a day of their birth, for example, but they will remain with their mothers for up to four years.

Above: Camels, as a group, first evolved in North America about 45 million years ago. Today's two species are found in the Old rather than the New World. They are recognizable by their humps.

Left: The dromedary, or Arabian camel, has just a single hump. It was first domesticated in central Asia, in the fourth century B.C., but now there are only about 500 wild dromedaries left in southwestern Mongolia and the northwest region of China.

Right: A group of bactrian camels cool off in a water hole under the hot desert sun. They can go for long periods without drinking. A camel in a good condition has a plump, upright, hump; in dehydrated or hungry animals, the humps sag.

Above: A female bactrian camel with several juveniles. The majority of offspring are born during March and April. Females normally produce a single youngster, but twins are known.

Above: A bactrian camel in Mongolia. When it sheds its winter coat, it takes on a very shaggy appearance.

Arabian camel
Camelus dromedarius

Bactrian camel
Camelus bactrianus

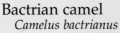

Distribution: North Africa and Asia.
Size: Up to 2.3m(7ft 7in) at the hump.
Pregnancy: Lasts 13-13.5 months.
Lifespan: Can be up to 50 years.
Conservation status: The Bactrian camel has declined in numbers.
Danger element: Generally bad-tempered, and can inflict a painful bite.

Right: Camels can carry loads of up to 270kg (595lb). Their milk is used to make kumiss, an alcoholic drink, and they are valued as well for their meat, hide and dung.

GUANACOS – WILD COUSINS OF THE LLAMA

This South American member of the camel clan differs from its relatives in Africa and Asia in lacking any trace of a hump. It is thought to be the wild ancestor of the llama, which was domesticated almost 5,000 years ago. There is another very similar species in South America, called the vicuna, and this is generally believed to be the original form of the domesticated alpaca.

When the Spanish invaders conquered the Incas in 1531, guanacos were very common, with a population which could have exceeded 50 million individuals. Since then, their numbers have fallen, with many being slaughtered for their pelts. The species is now protected throughout much of its range.

The guanaco and its relatives – known collectively as the llamoids – are well adapted to survive in their relatively inhospitable environment. They live at high altitudes, where the weather is cold and the air is thin. To compensate for the lower concentration of oxygen in the air, the haemoglobin in the red blood cells combines with oxygen more effectively than in mammals found at lower altitudes. There are also more blood cells, which increases the amount of oxygen the blood can carry but makes the blood thicker. In turn, the heart muscle is enlarged to pump this thicker blood around the body, where oxygen is released into the tissues. The dense furry coats of llamoids provide sound protection against the biting cold, while their sure-footed gait has made them invaluable beasts of burden, able to carry heavy packs through mountainous areas that no vehicle could reach.

Guanacos live in herds, usually made up of several females and a single male. When threatened, they escape by running at speeds of up to 64kph(40mph). They can also swim if necessary. Youngsters remain with the group until they are a year old, and are then driven out, to live alone until they join another group.

Above: An adult llama with her youngster. Llamas are thought to be the domesticated form of the guanaco and vary in colour.

Right: The guanaco is found in a range of habitats, from grassland to savanna, and can be encountered at altitudes up to 4,250m(13,900ft). It does not appear to need to drink, as its water requirement is met from its food, and it can wander without having to remain close to a source of water. It is a good swimmer and occasionally bathes in mountain streams.

Above: The natural habitat of guanacos and other llamoids is in the Andes of South America. Here, the nights are cold and the animals are protected by a thick coat. They have been hunted for their skins, which are used both as clothing and for making tents. Llamoids have thick blood to carry more oxygen and, like camels, have oval rather than round red blood cells.

Above: When they lie down, llamoids put their weight on their front legs, drop down onto their hindquarters, and then tuck their front feet under the body.

Below: Females breed every second year. Youngsters walk almost from birth, are suckled for up to 12 weeks and leave the herd at about one year old.

Right: The alpaca is highly valued for its coat of fine wool and has been specially bred for this feature. Fine alpaca robes were made for Inca kings.

Below: The Incas also valued the vicuna. Wild herds were rounded up and sheared but, since that time, their numbers have fallen dramatically.

Above: A group of guanacos in the Paine National Park, Chile. They live in herds of up to 10 females headed by a single male and sometimes migrate, but are frequently sedentary. They may have special dunging sites, up to 2.4m(8ft) in diameter.

Guanaco
Lama guanicoe

Distribution: Foothills of the Andes, from Peru, Chile and Argentina as far south as southern Patagonia.
Size: Stands up to 1.15m(3ft 9in) at the shoulder.
Pregnancy: Lasts 10-11 months.
Lifespan: Up to 28 years in captivity.
Conservation status: Under no immediate threat.
Danger element: Sufficiently amenable to have been domesticated.

MOOSE – THE LARGEST DEER

Moose are the largest deer in the world, and males have formidable antlers with a span that may be 2m (6ft 7in) from tip to tip. These are lost each December, and start to grow again about four months later. As the horns emerge, they are covered in furry velvet, which the animal rubs off on branches to reveal the brown horn beneath. By the time that the breeding season occurs in the autumn, the horns will have developed to their full extent, allowing males to fight each other for dominance. As with other deer, it is possible to age bulls approximately by the shape of their antlers. At the end of its first year, for example, a young male moose has simple straight antlers, measuring up to 15cm(6in) long, with no forks in them.

Unlike many deer, moose live on their own, rather than in herds. Females track males, and answer their calls during the breeding season. Following mating, the male may accompany the female until after she has given birth. Twins are common in females that have bred before. At first, the youngsters are slow to move, but as time goes by, they will walk rapidly alongside their mother.

A variety of predators threaten young moose, including wolves and bears, but although the female may lack horns, she is very fierce in defence of her offspring. A blow from her powerful feet can prove fatal to a wolf, for example, and once it is injured, the moose will then trample it to death. Older calves usually remain with their mother when she gives birth again, although gradually they will go their separate ways and start to breed in their own right.

Above: A bull moose in Denali National Park, Alaska, responds to the scent of a cow in breeding condition by curling his lips.

Left: Two bulls spar at the start of the mating period in autumn. These deer do not live in herds.

Right: Moose have no hesitation in taking to water and prove effective swimmers, if necessary.

Left: A bull moose, showing the huge antlers characteristic of these deer. The flap of skin hanging beneath the throat is often described as the 'bell'.

Above: A moose and her calf graze together. Adults eat about 19.5kg(43lb) of vegetation daily.

Below: A solitary cow moose drinking in a lake. Although groups sometimes congregate in suitable areas in the winter when food is scarce, they will not stay together subsequently.

Above: A young moose will be able to browse when it is just two weeks old. However, it will be suckled by its mother for a total of five months, and stays with her for more than a year.

Moose
Alces alces

Distribution: From northern Europe to eastern Siberia, Mongolia and Manchuria. Also present in Alaska, Canada and the northeastern United States. Introduced to New Zealand.
Size: Stands 1.68-2.3m(5ft 6in-7ft 7in) high at the shoulder; females smaller than males.
Pregnancy: About 35 weeks.
Lifespan: Up to 20 years.
Conservation status: Found over a wide area and not considered threatened.
Danger element: Females, in particular, can be aggressive in defence of their offspring.

REINDEER – TENACIOUS WORKHORSES OF THE NORTH

In contrast to most deer, reindeer cows have antlers, like bulls. This may well be a reflection of the inhospitable part of the world in which they live. In the autumn, at the end of the mating period (called the rut), the male reindeer shed their antlers. This means that the females, who retain their antlers for most of the year, are then the dominant herd members for a period. This gives them access to the best grazing sites through the bitterly cold winter, when food is sometimes in short supply. In this way, the cows are able to ensure grazing for their offspring, without fear of being displaced by larger stags.

During the winter months, the reindeer's coat becomes significantly paler in colour. This helps to conceal them from wolves and bears, their traditional enemies. Should they be sufficiently harassed, reindeer are powerful swimmers, and may take to icy waters to avoid such predators. As spring softens the harsh conditions, some reindeer wander through woodland areas as they move further north to tundra areas for the summer. Here they can graze on the mosses and other plants that are available for a short time each year.

Reindeer have tremendous reserves of stamina, and are known to be capable of pulling a 136kg(300lb) load for up to 160km(100miles) a day. In many parts of their range, they have been partially domesticated by the native peoples as working animals and as sources of fresh milk, meat and hides. Their bones are even used as needles. Unfortunately, this traditional link between reindeer and man has been disrupted in northern Europe by the Chernobyl nuclear power disaster of 1986. The resulting radioactivity has contaminated the reindeer moss, a type of lichen that forms a major part of their diet, and this in turn has concentrated the radioactivity within the reindeers' bodies to dangerous levels. The long-term effects on the reindeer population in this region are unclear.

Below: These deer used to have a much wider range, but have been eliminated from many parts of Europe. Often better known in North America as the caribou, this is the only species of deer in which both sexes have antlers on their heads.

Below: Reindeer have poor eyesight and rely on their hearing and keen sense of smell to escape danger. If threatened, they can run at 80kph(50mph).

Above: Reindeer are hardy animals, well adapted to life in a cold climate. Their hooves are flat and wide, with a deep cleft that allows them to walk in snow. For part of the year, they may congregate in huge herds of over 50,000 individuals.

Reindeer
Rangifer tarandus

Distribution: The far north of Europe and North America.
Size: Stands up to 1.27m(4ft 2in) high at the shoulder.
Pregnancy: Lasts 30-34 weeks.
Lifespan: Up to 15 years.
Conservation status: Relatively common, and semi-domesticated in some areas.

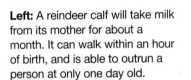

Left: A reindeer calf will take milk from its mother for about a month. It can walk within an hour of birth, and is able to outrun a person at only one day old.

Below: Males have longer antlers than females. These grow covered in a protective skin called velvet, which is rubbed off, revealing the antler beneath.

Above: Reindeer are important to the people who live in the far north. Domestication began about 3,000 years ago, but herds usually roam freely. This group has been rounded up.

GIRAFFES – THE TALLEST LIVING ANIMALS

The giraffe is the tallest living animal in the world today; the largest individual on record stood just over 5.8m(19ft) tall. Giraffes are found in areas of scrub and open woodland throughout much of Africa, south of the Sahara Desert. There are nine races, which can be separated on the basis of their height, markings, coloration and number of horns. The Masai giraffes, found in Tanzania and southern Kenya, tend to be the tallest, but in all cases females are smaller than males.

The great height of the giraffe does not result from any additional vertebrae in the neck, it is simply that these seven bones are greatly elongated. The long neck enables giraffes to browse on plants that are out of reach of most other animals except, perhaps, elephants. Giraffes spend most of their day feeding, and this activity continues through the night as well, especially when the moon is out. They may each consume up to 66kg(145lb) of vegetation every day. When giraffes need to drink, they approach a water hole and splay their front legs apart, bending their knees so that they can reach the water easily. The giraffe is almost unique among mammals in not being able to swim; they will never attempt to cross deep rivers for fear of drowning.

Giraffes live in loose herds, and there is rarely any conflict between individuals. A dominant male will mate with all the females in the area, and births take place in recognized calving areas within their territory. At birth, young bulls can be up to 1.9m(6ft 3in) tall and weigh 102kg(224lb). They are born with horns, which remain covered by skin throughout the animal's life. Females are very protective towards their calves, which are weaned by the time they are one and a half years old. Many young giraffes fall prey to hunting animals, particularly lions and African hunting dogs.

Right: The long neck of the giraffe enables these herbivores to feed on trees and shrubs that are out of reach to most other animals, except elephants.

Left: The two characteristic horns of the giraffe are more prominent in males than in females.

Left: Young male giraffes establish dominance by a necking match, as shown here. They intertwine their necks and then push each other from side to side until one submits.

Right: Drinking is an ungainly procedure for giraffes. It requires them to splay their legs and bend their knees in order to lower their heads to the water. The tail is an effective fly whisk.

Giraffe
Giraffa camelopardalis

Distribution: Occurs in Africa, south of the Sahara.
Size: Stands up to 5.8m(19ft).
Pregnancy: Lasts 15-15.5 months.
Lifespan: Up to 25 years.
Conservation status: Not uncommon.
Danger element: Defend by kicking.

Above: Giraffes live in loose groupings; cows generally range over an area of 120sq. km. (46sq. miles), while young bulls cover a much wider area. All will run at speed if danger threatens.

Left: A young giraffe with its mother. It faces many dangers from predators that roam the plains. Half of all calves born will live less than six months.

Right: Giraffes can eat thorny plants by producing large quantities of saliva, which allows the food to be swallowed without sticking in the mouth or throat. The roof of the mouth is also grooved and thickened.

WILDEBEESTS – THRONGING THE AFRICAN PLAINS

The two different species of wildebeest – the blue and the black – are both confined to Africa, where they flourish on the grassy plains. Wildebeests are members of the antelope family, although perhaps more reminiscent of cattle with their upturned horns. They graze on grass and other vegetation, and will sometimes also browse on bushes.

In certain parts of their range, where food is abundant, wildebeest are present throughout the year. Here, distinct single sex herds can be identified, with dominant males living a solitary existence, mating with females that enter their territories. Younger males, generally under four years old, live in bachelor groups, before establishing their own territories. Although they may use their horns, actual combat is rare, but males challenging for territories call loudly, with the sound 'genu' echoing across the plains (hence 'gnu' as the alternative common name). In other areas, herds are migratory, with huge numbers coming together and moving along well-trodden paths in search of food during the dry season.

The breeding period is also influenced greatly by the area concerned, with the single youngster being born at the start of the rainy season, just before the grass begins to grow again. Young wildebeests are born in a very advanced state of development, being able to stand within 15 minutes of birth and run shortly afterwards. This helps to ensure that as many as possible escape the clutches of lions and leopards.

Left: With its ears lowered, a wildebeest is courting a potential mate. No permanent pair bond is created within wildebeest populations, although certain bulls are dominant within their own area.

Although the blue wildebeest has remained common, numbers of the black wildebeest fell to the point of extinction because of heavy hunting at the turn of the century. Today, their numbers have built up again, and this species is no longer endangered.

Left: Locked in combat in the Amboseli National Park in Kenya, two male wildebeest battle each other for supremacy. Within the wildebeest hierarchy, bulls live in bachelor groups until they can establish their own individual territories.

Right: Wildebeest are usually found in areas of open grassland and often quite close to water. They are always alert, even at sunset, for fear of predators. If they are disturbed, they start pawing at the ground and then dash off some distance, before pausing again. They will use their horns to defend themselves if they are cornered.

Right: Although the mating season extends over a longer period, wildebeest calves in East Africa are generally born within a few weeks of each other. They can run virtually from birth, and with hundreds of individuals in a herd, some will survive this vulnerable stage.

Above: A wildebeest calf on its own. This individual has lost its mother, and will almost certainly fall victim to one of many predators.

Black wildebeest
Connochaetes gnou

Blue wildebeest
Connochaetes taurinus

Distribution: From southern Kenya southwards into South Africa.
Size: Ranges from 1.15m(3ft 9in) to 1.4m(4ft 7in) at the shoulder.
Pregnancy: Lasts 8-9 months.
Lifespan: Over 21 years in captivity.
Conservation status: In no danger of extinction.
Danger element: Females will seek to defend their calves.

Above: Part of a migrating group of wildebeest. During the dry season, huge herds made up of thousands of individuals move together across the plains in search of fresh grazing.

BUFFALO – BACK FROM THE BRINK

Huge herds of wild buffalo (bison) once thundered across the plains of North America, but the arrival of European settlers during the 1800s eventually caused their decline. Although hunted by the native Indians, the number they took posed no threat to the overall buffalo population, which numbered 50 million at its height. Then, as the railroad pushed west, it became fashionable to shoot buffalo from the trains. In the early stages of the slaughter, a single hunter might kill up to 100 buffalo a day. There were also large-scale hunts to feed the railroad construction workers and the settlers who followed this development. Some hunters, such as Buffalo Bill Cody, etched their names into the folklore of the developing nation. The scale of the slaughter can be best gauged by the fact that in 1889 the total number of buffalo left alive in North America was just 549. Thankfully, this tiny handful was protected, and the species is no longer considered to be in danger of extinction.

The European bison, sometimes called the wisent, has fared little better, also being reduced almost to extinction by hunting pressure. It is similar to the North American species in its habits, although it tends to be found more in forest than in open country. Here it grazes on the bark of trees, such as poplar, rather than on grasses, and seeks out acorns in the autumn.

Males in a group may fight each other to establish dominance, with such encounters being a fearsome sight, as they interlock their horns and battle to assert their strength. Calves tend to be born in the early spring, when food is more plentiful, and are guarded by the whole herd. They may face danger from packs of wolves, but are rarely molested by other animals.

Above: Nowadays, herds of buffalo are mainly confined to areas of national parkland, but at the start of the nineteenth century, millions of them roamed North America. The European bison is scarcer than its North American relative.

Left: Bison generally produce single calves. These weigh about 30kg(66lb) at birth and are capable of running after just a few hours. A mother will fiercely defend her offspring, charging with horns down at any potential predator that dares approach.

Right: Battling for supremacy, two bulls test their strength against each other. There is no overall dominant male within a herd; in fact, a number of the bulls will mate with cows. Once he has obtained a mate, the bull will stay close to her, driving off any challenger.

Above: The huge bulk of a mature male bison. This member of the cattle family can weigh up to 1,000kg(2,210lb). Native Indians relied upon buffalo for meat and hides.

Above: The difference in size between the sexes is clearly visible here, with a large bull standing alongside a cow. The horns and the prominent neck hump are also smaller in cows.

Below: This bison may be forced to browse on tree bark and twigs as it trudges through winter snow in the Yellowstone National Park. Herds move to higher ground in the spring.

American bison
Bison bison

European bison
Bison bonasus

Distribution: North America and eastern Europe.
Size: Stands up to 1.95m(6ft 5in) at the shoulder.
Pregnancy: Varies from 9 to 10 months.
Lifespan: Can be up to 20 years.
Conservation status: Their numbers are now stable.
Danger element: Sharp horns, coupled with massive bulk.

AMERICAN BEAVERS – INDUSTRIOUS DAM BUILDERS

After the capybara, American beavers are the second largest rodents in the world, and instantly recognizable by their broad, flat scaly tails. They live in groups of up to 12 individuals, and spend much of their time in water. The fur is covered in waterproofing oil and has a dense undercoat to provide further protection against the cold water. When diving, beavers close their nostrils and ears, and are able to stay submerged for as long as 15 minutes.

On land, beavers use their sharp teeth to gnaw down trees, which they use to build their characteristic dams. They can be surprisingly destructive; a single pair has been observed to fell 266 trees in a period of just 15 months as they constructed three separate dams, each measuring 15.2m(50ft) long. If they are left unmolested, successive generations of beavers may continue to develop a dam. The largest dam on record was built on the Jefferson River, Montana. It was 700m(2,300ft) long, and could be crossed on a horse.

In the quiet pool of water created by the dam, the beavers build a lodge with an underwater entry point. Each lodge is constructed to a similar pattern, using sticks and branches held together with mud, and forms a home for the beaver family. Mating takes place early in the year. Up to eight offspring may be born, each measuring about 38cm(15in) long, including their tails, and weighing about 0.45kg(1lb). The youngsters will start to eat bark, like adult beavers, from about a month old, and remain with their parents for at least two years. During this time, they will learn the intricate skills of constructing dams and lodges.

Left: Beavers live in small family groups, consisting of an adult pair and their offspring.

Left: Beavers are capable of inflicting considerable damage on areas of woodland. They feed on the bark of trees and also build dams with cut logs.

Above: The broad, flat tail of the beaver is used for steering, rather like a rudder, and can also be moved up and down to provide extra thrust in water.

Above: Having felled a tree, the beaver sets about cutting it into manageable lengths that can be dragged away and carefully added to its dam or lodge.

North American beaver
Castor canadensis

Distribution: North America, ranging from Alaska as far south as Tamaulipas in Mexico, and northern Florida.
Size: Up to 60cm(23in) at the shoulder.
Pregnancy: About 15 weeks.
Lifespan: Up to 15 years.
Conservation status: Reasonably common in suitable areas of habitat.
Danger element: Large incisor teeth have great destructive power. If a beaver dam bursts, surrounding land may flood.

Below: Beavers will readily take to water if they are threatened on land. Their coat is waterproof.

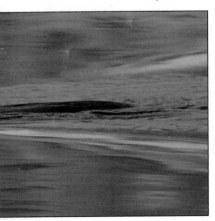

Left: The sharp incisor teeth of beavers are continually worn down by their gnawing activities.

Above: A young beaver being watched over by its parent. They may spend two years together.

BATS – AERIAL MASTERS OF THE NIGHT

This largely nocturnal group of mammals has successfully colonized most of the world, except for the far north. There are over 950 species, with the largest being the flying foxes found throughout much of the Pacific region. Their wingspan is at least 1.65m(5ft 5in) from tip to tip, and they can weigh over 1.38kg(3lb). In contrast, among the smaller species is the bumblebee bat of southwestern Thailand. Discovered in 1973, this bat has a very limited area of distribution, being known only from Kanchanburi province. Its total wingspan is just over 16cm(6.25in), and each adult weighs only 2gm(0.07oz). The lightest member of the group is Kitti's hognosed bat, with a wingspan of 15cm(6in) and weighing 1.5gm(0.05oz).

Bats feed on a variety of foods, with many catching flying insects after dark. Insectivorous bats are able to locate and track insects on the wing – as well as avoid obstacles – by using a system of echolocation. They emit ultrasonic calls, which are well above the range of human hearing, and use their sensitive ears to pick up the echoes bouncing off any objects in their path and build up a 'sound picture' of their environment. This system also enables blind bats to fly without difficulty.

While vast numbers of flying foxes can decimate fruit crops in tropical islands, the most notorious bat is the aptly named vampire. Armed with needle-sharp incisor teeth, vampire bats land on a sleeping victim, moving slowly over the body to find a warm area of skin where they can draw blood from vessels close to the surface. They lap up the blood from the open wound they make, aided by an anti-coagulant in their saliva that counteracts the victim's natural blood-clotting mechanism. In parts of Central and South America, where vampire bats are found, they are a major health threat because they can transmit the deadly rabies virus when they feed. As many as a million cattle and countless people die each year.

Right: Bats help in the distribution of fruit trees. Seeds swallowed by the bat pass through its body undigested and are voided in the faeces. Thus the seeds begin to grow in a new area, some distance away.

Below: Bats fly not by gliding, but by actively moving their wings. The thumb is positioned at the front of each wing, and the other four digits at the rear.

Above and right: Bats have evolved to take a wide variety of foods. The bulldog bat (above) eats mainly insects; a frog-eating bat is shown at right.

Left: A group of bats in a cave on the Indonesian island of Bali. The temperature inside the cave tends to remain quite stable, and thousands of bats may be found at such sites. By contrast, the large flying foxes prefer to congregate around exposed tree roots. Suitable sites may be used for many years.

Bats
Order Chiroptera

Distribution: Throughout the world on all continents, except for the far north and Antarctica.

Flying speed: Up to 64kph(40mph), by the Brazilian guano bat (*Tadarida brasiliensis*).

Pregnancy: May last 3-10 months.

Lifespan: About five years on average, but can be 30 years in some cases.

Conservation status: Some bats inhabit very small areas and are endangered. Many species are believed to be declining.

Danger element: The vampire bat may inject both animals and people with the fatal rabies virus as it feeds.

Above: The dreaded vampire bat is found in Central and South America. This nocturnal visitor feeds on blood and can transmit the fatal rabies virus as it does so. The deadly image of the vampire has been enshrined in a variety of horror films.

Below: When resting, bats will curl their wings tightly around their body, holding on upside down with their feet. This is a young short-nosed fruit bat from India, which roosts in the open.

KANGAROOS – UNIQUE POUCHED MAMMALS OF AUSTRALIA

The kangaroos are part of a group of marsupials, or pouched mammals, whose distribution is centred on Australia. They move mainly by hopping, their powerful hind limbs providing the thrust to enable them to leap distances of over 12.2m(40ft) and to clear obstacles up to 3m(almost 10ft) high. Kangaroos can also cover considerable distances, bounding at speeds of up to 40kph(25mph). On one memorable occasion, a kangaroo was pursued on horseback for about 30km(18.6 miles) and then leapt into the sea, swimming for a further 3km(1.7 miles).

The largest and one of the most widely distributed species is the red kangaroo, the males sporting distinctive reddish brown fur. Standing upright, a male may appear over 2.1m(6ft 11in) in height, with females being noticeably smaller. Kangaroos are browsing animals, feeding on grass and other vegetation. They can rapidly destroy pasture, grazing the grass lower than sheep, and are difficult to exclude from farmland, since the cost of secure fencing is prohibitive. In the past, the availability of water has tended to restrict the kangaroo's distribution, but now, with 'artificial' supplies provided for farm livestock, they have tended to increase in numbers, and culling programmes are now considered necessary to control their population in some parts of Australia.

As with other marsupials, the young kangaroo emerges into the world at a very early stage. Measuring less than 2.5cm(1in) long, it crawls into its mother's pouch and anchors itself to one of the teats. The youngster remains in the pouch for about eight months, after which it will make occasional return visits for a further six months until it is fully weaned.

Left: Kangaroos are able to travel at speed and jump obstructions readily, covering considerable distances in one leap. Their hind limbs move together, and the tail is held almost horizontally as a balance. Unfortunately, kangaroos have little road sense and frequently collide with vehicles at night.

Right: A joey peeps out from its mother's pouch. For many years, it was believed that the baby kangaroo was born in the pouch. Only in 1830 did a ship's surgeon discover that the birth took place normally, and that the tiny, almost helpless offspring then clambered instinctively up into the pouch. Even so, it was 1923 before this explanation of how a baby ended up in the pouch was finally accepted.